GRACE

Power Beyond
Your Ability

BY
DENNIS BURKE

Grace: Power Beyond Your Ability
ISBN 0-89274-904-0
© 1992 by Dennis Burke
P. O. Box 150043
Arlington, Texas 76015

Published by Harrison House, Inc.
P. O. Box 35035
Tulsa, Oklahoma 74153

CONTENTS

1 A COVENANT OF GRACE   5

2 STRONG IN GRACE   17

3 GRACE FOR GIVING   29

4 FALLEN FROM GRACE   43

5 STEWARDS OF GOD'S GRACE   55

6 SHOUT GRACE TO THE MOUNTAIN   67

1

A Covenant of Grace

Throughout the centuries of human history, God has remained committed to lifting His people out of the limits of their own ways and into the limitlessness of His great ability.

He joins Himself with His people through covenant. A covenant joins two parties together and brings the strengths and weaknesses of each into the other's situation. When, through simple faith, you entered the kingdom of God and the salvation of Jesus Christ, you also embraced the covenant foundation on which this kingdom operates.

As the Body of Christ understands the power of covenant life with God, they will step out of weakness and defeat and into the victories Jesus obtained for them.

The Old Covenant depended upon the Israelites' obedience to the laws and commands of God. The people's faith was in God Who made those laws. This covenant gave them a hold on Him as the covenant-keeping God.

In Deuteronomy 7:9, Moses told the people, "Know, therefore, that the Lord thy God, He is God, the faithful God, who keepeth covenant and mercy with them who love Him and keep His commandments...."

God revealed Who He is and also how firm His commitment was. In Isaiah 54:10, He said, "For the mountains shall depart, and the hills be removed; but My kindness shall not depart from thee, neither shall the covenant of My peace be removed...." His kindness and mercy toward you are more established than the mountains.

In Jeremiah 32:40, God spoke of the new covenant which would come: " I will make an everlasting covenant with them, that I will not turn away from them, to do them good; but I will put my fear in their hearts, that they shall not depart from me."

Again in Ezekiel 36:26-27, He looked ahead to this New Covenant:

A new heart also will I give you, and
a new spirit will I put within you,
and I will take away the stony heart

out of your flesh, and I will give you an heart of flesh. And I will put My spirit within you, and cause you to walk in My statutes, and ye shall keep My judgments, and do them.

His covenant would ultimately bring His influence and presence from dwelling *among* men to dwelling *within* them.

The old covenant was established on the earth by the blood of bulls and goats. The new covenant was established in heaven and on earth forever by the blood of the Lord Jesus Christ. The power of this covenant is no less than the power of the blood by which it was established.

In this new covenant, obedience in faith remains vital. But now it is faith springing from a heart that delights in obedience, and has the power to be obedient.

God gives His greatness and grace to all who come to Him in simple faith. His covenant is a covenant of grace. He is a God of grace, and He imparts grace to all who will enter into His covenant.

The word "grace" is used primarily in two different ways. First, it is central to the heart attitude of God which moves Him toward people. Because of God's grace, He is willing to be involved with you and me. He gives His love and resources freely, not on the basis of performance. That love is not swayed by what you do, or what you don't do. He loves you regardless of your actions, just because you are His child.

Second, grace is the power which is active within the heart of the believer, and that works in him, empowering him to do God's will.

If ever man had a need, it is for the grace of God. From the most talented person to the one who feels least qualified, grace from God is desperately needed.

The natural mind wants to feel self-sufficient, capable of handling anything. The truth is that each of us is inadequate in many areas of life.

The successful businessman may lack the skills to influence his family and develop a warm and loving home. A wife may be a good homemaker, yet come short of the spiritual strength needed for a stable household. Even good people, faithful to their church, can fail miserably at living in the power of the Holy Spirit as the Word of God teaches.

Jesus Christ has uncovered the path into the very strength and ability of God to empower you for any task before you. That path is found in the covenant of grace.

God has made Himself available to supply all people with the ability to do His will and enjoy His blessing. His grace can enable you to accomplish in life the things that God demands in His Word. He has longed to remove from you the limits of sin and sensuality, and open to you the riches of grace.

Through sin, Satan has kept people bound inside the realm of their own reason and flesh. The continual bombardment of ideas and attitudes from a world governed by sin presses to penetrate the life of every person. You find the things on the outside always trying to invade your mind and body.

Jesus came to deliver you from those limits and to deposit His Spirit within you to influence and lead you: "But if the Spirit of Him who raised Jesus from the dead dwells in you, He who raised Christ from the dead will also give life to your mortal bodies through His Spirit who dwells in you" (Romans 8:11, NKJV).

God has placed within us the seeds of His kingdom and made us alive in the inner man of the heart.

Now you can live from the inside out. You are free to affect the conditions and environment around you with the power of His Word that has its home within your heart.

When God entered into a covenant with Abraham, the father of faith, He set in motion the events that would bring Jesus Christ and the redemption of all mankind into this world. Today you and I have been given the privilege of living in fellowship with the Almighty God and walking in the grace He continually provides.

This covenant of grace is not like the law of the Old Covenant. All of the benefits of this covenant are received by faith. They cannot be earned or merited. It is by faith and faith alone that you enter this covenant with God: "For by grace have you been saved through faith, and that not of yourselves; it is the gift of God" (Ephesians 2:8, NKJV).

Salvation is more than going to heaven after you die. The inheritance Jesus gives is yours after His death on the cross, not after your death. That means all of His inheritance is yours *now*.

Before the sacrifice of Jesus, the people looked ahead to the promise of God which was to come. Now we look back to the promise which was established for us. Faith does not look at the blessing which will come one day. It sees the Word of God which has been given and established through Jesus. The promises are linked to your covenant and belong to you now.

Salvation is wholeness—spirit, soul and body. Our wholeness is received through faith. But it is by the grace of God at work within us. Notice Hebrews 4:1,9-11(NKJV):

> Therefore since a promise remains of entering His rest, let us fear lest any of you seem to have come short of it. There remains therefore a rest for the people of God. For he who has entered His rest has himself also ceased from his own works as God did from His. Let us therefore be diligent to enter that rest, lest anyone fall after the same example of disobedience.

There is a promise of rest in God that releases His power when we diligently trust in His power and not our own. It is faith in the deposit of grace and ability He has placed within our inner man.

Disobedience kept Israel from entering the territory promised to them. Their example of unbelief demonstrates how faith must be mixed with the promise of God to obtain the results He has offered.

In Hebrews 4:3 is a powerful truth: "For we who have believed do enter that rest, as He has said: So I swore in My wrath, They shall not enter My rest, although the works were finished from the foundation of the world."

Paul said, "The works were finished!" The work was finished before Israel faced the wilderness or the enemies who lived in their promised land. God had already completed the necessary works for them to enter peacefully and at rest.

The work for their victory and yours was completed before the world was established. God's last day of work was Adam's first day of life.

God's work in the physical world was finished at creation. His work in the spiritual world was finished through the death, burial and resurrection of the Lord Jesus.

You have been created to live in God's rest. He has created everything for you. The work was God's part. Entering His rest is your part. You must be diligent that your effort is in entering His rest, not in continuing in your own works or strength.

You are to live by grace, not by your own works and ambition. The works were finished at the foundation of the world. Everything now must be founded upon His work and your diligence to enter His rest.

Under the Old Covenant, the priests were forbidden to wear anything which would cause sweat as they served before the altar (Ezekiel 44:18). Sweat is a symbol of the curse (Genesis 3:17-19). God has provided the grace and ability to fulfill His work with His strength.

In Matthew 11:28-30 (NKJV), Jesus said:

Come to Me, all you who labor and are heavy laden, and I will give you rest. Take My yoke upon you and learn from Me, for I am gentle and lowly in heart, and you will find rest for your souls. For My yoke is easy and My burden is light.

Notice, first He promises rest to those who bring their load of care to Him. This is imparted rest, freely given to anyone who will receive.

Then He tells how to find rest. This rest is learned by taking *His* yoke upon you. This is the lasting rest which enables you as His disciple to continually handle the weight and the work by drawing on the resource of His strength.

Jesus said that this ability to find lasting rest comes by taking His yoke. The picture He paints is of a double yoke for using two oxen to plow a field.

When a farmer trained a young ox, he yoked him to an older, fully-trained ox. That young ox may have wanted to run to the right or left or even lie down. But the yoke on his neck that linked him to that older ox held him to the speed and direction which the old ox knew was best.

When your life comes under the lordship of God, and His Word becomes the final authority to you, where and how fast you go will be determined by Him and not by you.

Jesus taught that this is the key to lasting rest and the power to produce results.

The rest He imparts is wonderful for the immediate relief of some terrible situation. But the real disciple lives not for those imparted moments of rest, but for the life of rest that is learned and embraced.

Living by the covenant of grace—in which His strength is governing and directing you—is the key to bringing glory to Jesus and not yourself. Your part is to enter into His works and learn the laws of His kingdom.

It all begins with a covenant, the covenant of grace.

2
Strong in Grace

The real strength of the message of Jesus is not man's ability in himself, but his potential in Christ Jesus. God has made us in His image and likeness to reveal His goodness and to show His greatness in human form. Jesus Himself is our picture of the goodness of God in action. He went about doing good and healing all that were oppressed of the devil (Acts 10:38).

The apostle Paul becomes for us the example of a man redeemed from a life of sin against God, who turns his world right side up with the power of this gospel.

In Paul's writings, he points to the most vital aspect of the message he has been given. Every one of his letters refers to grace from our Lord Jesus Christ.

Grace. It is the most vital subject. It is at the heart of all that God is doing in humanity. Yet, it remains a sometimes vague and neglected subject. We assume that everyone understands what grace is.

Two aspects of grace must be seen. First, it is the gracious heart of God the Father that moves Him to love us and lift our lives into His best. His grace looks beyond our sin and shortcomings and sees us in the light of forgiveness through the sacrifice of Jesus.

Though we could never earn His blessings through our own good deeds, He has chosen to freely bless our lives.

Second, grace is the power of God at work in you to fulfill what He has designed.

Strong's Exhaustive Concordance defines grace as "the divine influence [of God] upon the heart, and its reflection in the life."

Grace is God's ability in you to do what you cannot do on your own. The Apostle Paul said, "By the grace of God I am what I am..." (1 Corinthians 15:10).

What you become for God will be the result of *His* grace and ability.

In 2 Timothy 2:1 Paul says, "Thou therefore, my son, be strong in the grace that is in Christ Jesus." We must be strong in His grace.

In his book, *Covenant and Blessings,* Andrew Murray says, "Grace is not only the power that moves the heart of God in its compassion toward us, when He acquits and accepts the sinner and makes him a child. It is also the power that moves the heart of the saint and provides it each moment with just the disposition and the power which it needs to love God and do His will."

It is important to see God's grace as a power in your life. It is the power within to bring change. If you can be changed by God's influence on the inside, you can be more effective in bringing change to situations on the outside.

Faith changes things. God has given you His faith to grow in and bring change to the natural situations you face. He works together with you to bring His power and influence for those outer changes.

Grace changes people. By God's grace you become what He has said in His Word you will be.

You may be facing the most challenging problem. You feel that you cannot cope with the pressure. Yet, you know that God has provided you with all of the power and ability to handle any situation.

The grace you have had does not seem to be enough. Your weakness and inability seem to contain you and threaten your faith.

You must do what the Apostle Peter said, "grow in grace" (2 Peter 3:18).

The gospel of Matthew gives one of the clearest pictures of this need for grace:

Then cometh Jesus with them unto a place called Gethsemane, and saith unto the disciples, Sit ye here, while I go and pray yonder. And he took with him Peter and the two sons of Zebedee, and began to be sorrowful and very heavy. Then saith he unto them, My soul is exceedingly sorrowful, even unto death; tarry ye here and watch with me. And he went a little further, and fell on his face, and prayed, saying, O my Father, if it be possible, let this cup pass from me; nevertheless, not as I will, but as thou wilt. And he cometh unto the disciples, and findeth them asleep; and he saith unto Peter, What, could ye not watch with me one hour? Watch and pray, that ye enter

not into temptation; the spirit indeed
is willing, but the flesh is weak.
(Matthew 26:36-41).

Jesus went into the garden to pray with a
heaviness that seemed as though it would
kill Him. He was facing the darkest moment
in human history. He prayed that this cup
would pass from Him if possible. His flesh
drew back from the impending lashes of the
whip on His back, just as yours would.

When He entered the garden, He wanted
His closest followers with Him. He wanted
their support and prayer during the most
difficult task that a man ever confronted.

Three times, He prayed a prayer of
commitment. He was willing to do what
was necessary. But the sense of power
and authority is distinctly absent from
these prayers. You can feel the heaviness
in His voice. You can hear the weakness
of His humanness.

When he told Peter, "The spirit indeed is
willing, but the flesh is weak," He was
speaking not only of the disciples' weakness,
but also of His own.

Jesus has lived life in the weakness of
flesh. He knows and understands the limits

that your body and emotions constantly try to impose on you. But He shows us how to rise above the limits of our humanness and how to live by the power of the inner, spirit man.

Notice verses 45-46. There is a difference in Jesus' voice:

" Sleep on now, and take your rest. Rise, let us be going..."

Something has happened! When Jesus entered the garden, He wanted the disciples to stay awake and pray with Him. Then He released them to sleep. Now, in a bold declaration He says, "Rise."

John 18 tells of the Roman soldiers coming at this point to seek Jesus. When He said, "I am He," they fell to the ground *under the power of God*.

This is no longer the weak, heavy Jesus Who entered the garden. There has been a change. Jesus walks into the plan for man's redemption with total control and complete submission to the will of His heavenly Father.

What made the difference in the garden? Hebrews 4:16 gives the answer: " Let us therefore, come boldly unto the throne of grace, that we may obtain mercy, and find grace to help in time of need."

Jesus came to the throne of grace and found the strength and ability to do what he could not do in Himself. He chose to rely on His heavenly Father, just as you and I must. He demonstrated how to face adversity through the power of the Holy Spirit. He knew what it was to feel the limitations of flesh. He was tempted in every way as we are, yet He did not let His weakness dominate Him (Hebrews 4:15). He came into the presence of His Father and found all that He needed (Hebrews 4:16).

Weakness is not sin. But to try to excuse disobedience because of *human* weakness is sin.

You have open access to the very presence and throne of God. You are invited to come boldly to the throne of God's grace and find the strength and ability *you* need.

God's Word says, "So then faith cometh by hearing, and hearing by the word of God" (Romans 10:17). If faith grows by hearing the Word of God, then how does grace grow? Grace grows by finding the presence of God and entering into it.

The Holy Spirit has placed a high priority on prayer. It is in the personal times of prayer that we come to His throne. There is a clear message to the Church that God wants us in His presence daily. The outgrowth of this renewed emphasis on prayer is that God's own people are growing in His grace.

A throne is a place of authority. You have been given the right and privilege to come into the highest place of authority in the universe. As you approach God confidently, you can be filled with *His* confidence and inner ability to stand firm on His promise. His authority will rise within you to *do* His will. You will not stand in your own strength or authority, but in His.

You must see in your life the relationship of this grace with faith. Faith changes things. You know situations arise that you do not really have faith to see changed. Or there are aspects of the path where God has placed you that you seem unable to follow.

If God has truly directed you, certainly He knows whether you can succeed. But the question is not if you have the natural ability for the task, but rather, if you have the grace.

God does not call us to do only what we are capable of doing. In fact, He calls people to do what they cannot do. If a person is doing for God only what he can do, then he is possibly not fulfilling his calling.

Anything that is done for God apart from His grace is dead works. Second Timothy 2:5 makes it clear: "A man who enters an athletic contest wins no prize unless he keeps the rules laid down" (Phillips).

When God calls you into His plan, it is not your talent or intelligence in which He is interested. He looks specifically for those who will do His will regardless of their personal ability.

The Apostle Paul is a great example. He was a man respected among the religious leaders in Israel. As a Pharisee taught by the great Gamaliel, he would seem the likely choice to present the gospel of Jesus to the most influential Jews. God did not, however, send Paul to Israel, but to the Gentile world. God sent him where his religious background was of little importance. He would need to rely on the Holy Spirit to fulfill God's plan.

Whatever you are commissioned to do in the kingdom of God, to fulfill it you will need the grace that comes from time spent in His presence.

Many are disappointed because they have directed their prayer and their faith to bring about a change, but have failed to see any real result.

So many times, people try to use faith to change something, but they lack the level of inner ability to sustain the faith they are using. They are reaching out in faith, when first they need to grow in *grace*.

Grace is the inner substance that will sustain you as you apply the principles of faith to change things. If you give up on the inside, you will faint on the outside.

Faith overcomes the problems. Grace keeps the problems from overcoming you.

Growing in grace enables you to enter into greater and greater dimensions of power in your inner man and then greater results of releasing that power through prayer.

Hebrews 12:28 says, "Wherefore, receiving a kingdom which cannot be moved, let us have grace, by which we may serve God acceptably with reverence and godly fear."

Acceptably means according to God's ability. The service to God that truly honors Him is not accomplished by talent or determination alone. It must be done in His strength and ability.

Come into His presence and grow in grace. Let His ways become your ways, and His thoughts become your thoughts. As you do, His ability will emerge from within, and you will see a new strength in His grace.

3

Grace for Giving

There is an evidence of God working within the heart of a believer. It can be seen in the earliest accounts of the Church as the Holy Spirit began to bring them together as a body of people.

In Acts 4, the Apostles Peter and John were arrested after the healing of the crippled man who was begging at the gate called Beautiful. They were brought before the council and religious leaders where they were examined and threatened because of the great stir that had resulted from this miracle.

When they were released, they returned to the others among them and told of the events that had taken place. They joined together in one spirit and prayed for God to use them and show Himself strong through them.

After they had prayed, there was a powerful move of God through them as is recorded.

Notice verse 33: "And with great power gave the apostles witness of the resurrection of the Lord Jesus; and great grace was upon them all."

There was an immediate manifestation of God in them that would establish them as a powerful witness of Jesus Christ. The grace of God was evident upon all.

This grace from God was His favor and blessing toward them. It was His influence in their hearts and the imparting of His ability empowering them to do what they are unable to do on their own.

The first thing they did as God's grace was upon them is described in the following verses:

Neither was there any among them that lacked; for as many as were possessors of lands or houses sold them, and brought the prices of the things that were sold, and laid them down at the apostles' feet; and distribution was made unto every man according as he had need (Acts 4:34-35).

There was a wonderful spirit of generosity that spread among the entire

Church. They began to give for the advancement of the gospel and for *meeting the needs* of other people.

That generosity was the result of the grace of God at work within the heart to become a giver. Possessions begin to lose their grip as you grow in grace.

God is the greatest giver there is, and as His heart is born into you and matures in you, His same motivation becomes important to you. Giving is a lifestyle that is at the very heart of Christianity. It is evident in the Church from the beginning and is intended to increase in us today.

It is an area that can be so misunderstood or used for wrong, self-serving reasons that many ministers and leaders choose to leave it completely alone. But if God's Word gives us an example to live by, we must teach it and proclaim it in the way that God has intended. Then we can know that it will not be taught to manipulate people, but rather to minister to them and bring godly increase into their lives.

The Apostle Paul points to the church of Macedonia as an example of the kind of giving that pleases God, advances the kingdom of God, and activates the blessing of God in the personal lives of believers.

Notice 2 Corinthians 8:2-7 from *The Heart of Paul*, the Ben Campbell Johnson paraphrase of Paul's letters:

> In the midst of their suffering, their deep joy and their poverty inspired them to give liberally to others. I witness to the fact that according to their ability - yes, even beyond their ability - they gave of their own free will. They literally begged us to take their money and take responsibility for distributing it to Christpersons in need. And contrary to our expectations they had their giving in proper priority. First, they gave themselves to God and then contributed to us according to his will. Now I had urged Titus, who had begun teaching you how to give, to help you mature in giving. Just as you have abounded in all the gifts like faith, the power to speak, knowledge, your love for us, and in deep desire, I hope you will also abound in giving.

Here is a church that had experienced great hardships. They were suffering and under persecution for their faith in Jesus. Yet, in the times of trouble and poverty, there was an attitude of giving that emerged as an example to the Church for all ages.

How could people be so motivated to give when they faced poverty themselves? How could they have joy in giving when there was such hardship?

When you come to believe the covenant promises that are linked with honoring God with your wealth, you can easily understand their joy and giving. They were acting in faith to promote the kingdom of God with their wealth and receive the increase which God commands on all who will give with the right heart.

They were inspired to give by the promise of God. They were giving to the poor though they were poor themselves. Because Proverbs 19:17 says, "He that hath pity upon the poor lendeth unto the Lord; and that which he hath given will he pay him again."

When you are facing lack of any kind, you can activate the promise of God by giving according to the Word of God. You can literally give your way out of lack. That was one of the things that inspired this church in Macedonia to give, as well as the needs of those to whom they were giving.

In the mind of the Apostle Paul, this was such a vital subject that he left Titus in the city with them to teach them and help them mature in giving.

Notice again the way he said it in 2 Corinthians 8:7 (HOP): "Just as you have abounded in all gifts... I hope you will also abound in giving." *God's way to increase is giving.* It is contrary to the world's mentality of increase. In natural thinking, the only way to increase is to get. In God's economy it is to give.

Of course, the priority in your life must be in harmony with God's. Paul said of this example church in Macedonia, "...they had their giving in the proper priority. First, they gave themselves to God and then contributed to us according to his will" (verse 5, HOP).

The heart's desire of God's people is not to gain wealth for their own lusts, but rather to minister to the needs of people in every area of life. It is important to have the money necessary to help those in need, to have the funds to underwrite a mission project, or to be able, for example, to help support a home for unwed mothers.

There are many desperate needs that require godly people with the wealth and faith to minister to them. I believe God will help you to rise up and increase in order to do your part as a giver to the ministry.

There are many critics of this sort of teaching. There have been abuses and even those who have used manipulation to persuade people to fund their own ideas rather than those of the Spirit of God. That is why true Bible teaching is so vital. When God's people grow up and truly respond to Him in their giving, the ungodly and disobedient will no longer get their hands on the money of the saints of God.

God has promised that He will cause us to increase. In the context of this portion of scripture, Paul said, "For you know the grace of our Lord Jesus Christ, that though He was rich, yet for your sake He became poor, that you through His poverty might become rich" (2 Corinthians 8:9, NAS).

The richness Paul is dealing with is not only spiritual. The context of this entire chapter is the money that *these people* would give as well as the result of God bringing His increase into every area of their lives.

God said that He wanted them to become rich, and that would include finances. That means more than enough to do anything they needed to do.

Now look at the apostle's recommendation:

Here now is my advice. About a year ago you were eager to make an offering, but you never finished making it. It is now time for you to complete it. You must match your inner willingness with your outward behavior by completing it according to what you have (2 Corinthians 8:10-11, HOP).

Match your inner willingness with your outward actions. It is time to reach out in your giving in order to do two things. First, to minister to the needs of people who need the gospel. Second, to begin to increase as you never have before.

In the Gospel of Luke, Jesus taught a parable that clearly links a person's money with the effectiveness he will have in other things:

He who is faithful in a very little thing is faithful also in much; and he who is unrighteous in a very little thing is unrighteous also in much. If therefore you have not been faithful in the use of unrighteous mammon, who will entrust the true riches to you? (Luke 16:10-11, NAS).

The true riches are the souls of people. How can you be trusted with people if you are unwilling to deal with money in a godly way? Trustworthiness, according to Jesus, is demonstrated by your willingness to subject your money to God's laws.

When you give as He has taught, then you will increase not only in your wealth financially, but also in your influence toward people.

It is so important for the Body of Jesus Christ to realize that we must handle the wealth of this world in order to reach this world. The revival we are entering is of such a great magnitude that believers everywhere are going to be required to grow in all aspects in order to participate. That will certainly mean financial growth.

The prophet Haggai spoke of this revival of the nations:

...Yet once, it is a while, and I will shake the heavens, and the earth, and the sea, and the dry land; and I will shake all nations, and the desire of all nations shall come: and I will fill this house with glory, saith the Lord of hosts. The silver is mine, and the gold is mine, saith the Lord of hosts. The glory of this latter house shall be greater than of the former, saith the Lord of hosts: and in this place will I give peace, saith the Lord of hosts (Haggai 2:6-9).

God declares that His glory will be revealed in the nations. In the middle of this prophecy He speaks of the silver and the gold being His. It may first seem to be out of place, but then you see that for the nations to be affected, and for the glory of God to be revealed in the house of God, the gold and silver must be moved out of the hands of the nations—the world—and into the hands of His nation, the Church.

There is a shifting of wealth ahead in the earth. Wealth is to come into the hands of godly men and women who will bring glory to God with it. The wealth of this earth is not here to satisfy the lusts and greed of the perverted. It is here to bring the freedom of Jesus Christ to the nations. It is to bring glory to God.

If you will not be afraid of the responsibility of wealth, God will show you how to increase in a greater measure.

Too many people have put the responsibility for their development and advancement in the hands of God, when He has clearly put it in their hands.

Galatians 6:7 says it this way: "A man's harvest in life will depend entirely on what he sows" (Phillips).

The context of this verse is the money given to those who teach the Word of God. You establish your own harvest by your giving to God's work.

In Galatians 6:8 Paul says, "For he that soweth to his flesh shall of the flesh reap corruption; but he that soweth to the Spirit shall of the Spirit reap life everlasting."

Certainly, this verse reaches beyond the financial realm. But the context is regarding giving. Our giving and honoring God with tithes and offerings is sowing to the spirit. *Your money reaches into the spirit realm!*

You can see this in the words of the angel of the Lord sent to Cornelius who had honored God:

> There was a certain man in Caesarea called Cornelius, a centurion of the band called the Italian band, a devout man, and one that feared God with all his house, which gave much alms to the people, and prayed to God alway. He saw in a vision evidently about the ninth hour of the day an angel of God coming in to him, and saying unto him, Cornelius. And when he looked on him, he was afraid, and said, What is it, Lord? And he said unto him, Thy prayers and thine alms are come up for a memorial before God (Acts 10:1-4).

Here is a man hungry for the reality of God, reaching out in the only way he knew. *He prayed and he gave.* The angel said that his praying and giving had built a memorial before God. He had entered into the spirit realm with prayer and giving. The money he gave went up before God in the Spirit and became an evidence of his hunger and honor for God.

His faith and hunger for God resulted in the Apostle Peter receiving a vision that commissioned him to bring the gospel to the Gentiles as well as to the Jews (Acts 10:9-48).

Your praying and giving in faith bring your needs into the presence of God. It is the very evidence that you are looking to Him and not to your own ability to meet your needs or change your circumstances. When you honor Him, He will direct you and guide your steps.

There is a final aspect of what your giving will do that I must include here. In 2 Corinthians 9:6-8, the Holy Spirit through Paul summarizes this principle:

> ...He which soweth sparingly shall reap also sparingly; and he which soweth bountifully shall reap also bountifully. Every man according as he purposeth in his heart, so let him give; not grudgingly, or of necessity: for God loveth a cheerful giver. And God is able to make all grace abound toward you; that ye, always having sufficiency in all things, may abound to every good work.

Paul said that all grace would abound toward *you*. The various aspects of grace, that bring God's ability to you for any area of life, will increase according to your giving and sowing into the kingdom of God. That puts the growth and advancment in your life within your influence. Your willingness to honor God with your wealth, and to reach out in faith to give, brings you to a place of God's ability multiplying on your behalf.

To say it once again, Galatians 6:7 in the Phillips translation is the most powerful and clear summary of this entire subject: "A man's harvest in life will depend entirely on what he sows."

Your harvest can change if you will choose to sow the right seeds. Let God's grace for giving be multiplied in you.

4

Fallen From Grace

When the Apostle Paul wrote to the church at Galatia, he addressed a problem which arises to challenge the Body of Christ in many ways. He urged the young church to correct an error to which they had yielded: the mistaken belief that their position with God and the power to do His will were based upon keeping the law and not on His grace.

In Galatians 1:6 Paul writes, "I marvel that ye are so soon removed from him that called you into the grace of Christ unto another gospel."

The Judaizers were Jews who had accepted Christianity, but believed that salvation was for the Jews only. They taught that for a Gentile to enter into the gifts and promises of God, he had to first become a Jew - man's salvation then depended on his obeying the law of Moses, as well as trusting in the sacrifice of Jesus. In contrast, Paul's message was that God's promise and power were the result of grace, and grace alone.

When James 2:17 speaks of works, they are the actions that spring from the Word and from a heart in right-standing with God. The works do not *give* you position with God. Instead, they *reveal* the place of power you have in Him.

There is a tendency in Christian life to lean on your own ability to accomplish God's plans, rather than on His ability. As I work with believers, I am often amazed by the traps that ensnare people who earlier had been close to God.

Any strategy of Satan becomes effective only when people fail to continue in God's strength and grace. They take matters into their own hands, facing their situations without the power of God's Word truly active in them. From the newest Christian to the seasoned saint, these tricks of Satan can pull people away from true power, and focus them on human effort.

Later in his appeal to the Galatians, Paul says, "Christ is become of no effect unto you, whosoever of you are justified by the law; ye are fallen from grace" (Galatians 5:4). Fallen from grace! To fall from grace is to allow God's grace to become null and void, to trust in something other than God's ability to accomplish His work or will. The J.B. Phillips translation of this verse reads, "...you put yourself outside the range of His grace."

A subtle process draws us away from the grace of God. His grace empowers us to do God's will, God's way. But without a fresh and strong dependence on His grace within, we will begin to look to other ways of fulfilling the desires of our heart.

To fall from grace is to work to do God's will without having the power alive and active in us that is necessary for the job. It is to live by laws, rules and human effort, without the deep awareness and trust that all is accomplished by grace, through faith.

It can also be seen when we are pushing to do what *we* want, regardless of *God's desire* for us. Ambition can be very deceptive. Ambition is directed by things *we* want to accomplish. Lacking God's blessing, we will need to complete those tasks with our own talents and abilities.

In our society, *each of us* must be a "person on the go" to keep up with the expectations for excelling. From our youth we are conditioned to think that education and hard work are the important ingredients for success. While these are certainly helpful, they are meaningless if not directed by the influence of the Holy Spirit.

Vision, on the other hand, is that which can be accomplished only with God's help and strength. He places His desire within your heart, and then your desire is centered on what He wants. God gives grace to those with vision—His vision!

Many people have fastened their ambition on a vision God gave to someone they admire. To the person with vision, God's provision and grace are abundant. But the one who pursues it as his own goal has to do it alone.

That is not to say that good things have not been done by ambitious people. I have known many whose personal drive produced impressive results. Even ministries have erected great buildings and completed notable projects by hard work and human ambition. But if mere ambition and human effort bring achievement, it will take more of the same to sustain it.

Success in the kingdom of God is measured by a standard different from the world's. Success in His kingdom is based solely on Who has told you to do what you are doing. God's blessing does not rest on your ambitious accomplishments, but on the vision He gives you.

When God has given you His vision, He supplies you with the grace to fully accomplish His plan and sustain it.

James 4:6 says, "...God resisteth the proud, but giveth grace unto the humble." When you humbly receive His desire, and pursue His plan with all of your heart, He will provide the grace and ability to see it through. Your only interest is that Jesus receives the glory.

The proud think more of their accomplishments than God's. They point more to themselves than to Jesus. They give you their opinions, rather than God's Word.

The proud can never grow. Yet they are unaware of their immaturity. They distance themselves from those who could speak wisdom into their lives, because they cannot admit they need anyone.

Unapproachable and unteachable, prideful people listen only to those who agree with them. Their accomplishments are their evidence of success. They must prove they are great so that people can marvel.

Anyone with the slightest perception can see their pride. It comes through in their words, their decisions and their actions. Many times God will send His appointed ministers to help open their eyes. He will stir His Word within them to free them from the limits of their own ambition and strength. But without the humility to receive this ministry, all will be ignored or refused.

God's grace comes to the humble: those who will exalt His Word, His will and His ways, those whose real meat is to do His will, regardless of applause (John 4:34). Success to them is in reaching out to do what God desires.

They know unquestionably that they cannot complete their task by themselves. They must receive His grace to do their work for Him. They must walk close to Him and have His words as their food.

The Apostle Paul clearly shows his reliance on this grace. Notice 1 Corinthians 15:10: "But by the grace of God I am what I am: and his grace which was bestowed upon me was not in vain; but I laboured more abundantly than they all: yet not I, but the grace of God which was with me."

Paul was confident in the grace within him. Yet he pointed to the grace of God as his strength, and his own labor as the fruit of God's gift to him.

How refreshing it is to be with those who live in this grace. You notice it in their words, their priorities and their interests. The world's standards do not dictate or even influence their goals. Their will is to do the will of their Father in heaven.

In Luke 6:30-34, Jesus taught about this attitude of grace:

> Give to every man that asketh of thee; and of him that taketh away thy goods ask them not again. And as ye would that men should do to you, do ye also to them likewise. For if ye love them which love you, what thank have ye? for sinners also love those that love them. And if ye do good to them that do good to you, what thank have ye? for

sinners also do even the same. And if ye lend to them of whom ye hope to receive, what thank have ye? for sinners also lend to sinners, to receive as much again.

In this passage, the word *thank* is from the same Greek word elsewhere translated *grace*. Jesus is teaching on the attitude of those who live by His grace.

If everything you do is for those who will do the same back to you, there is no grace needed. You draw upon His grace only when you reach beyond human ability to give, love and do good to others— without seeking a return from them. You look only to God for the rewards of your willingness to obey.

Jesus went on to say in Luke 6:35, "But love ye your enemies, and do good, and lend, hoping for nothing again; and your reward shall be great, and ye shall be the children of the Highest...."

The grace of the Father is seen in His children. The seed you plant in those who cannot repay will be rewarded by God Himself. But most important will be the picture of the heavenly Father that you present. He is a giver, and you have made that known.

Hebrews 10:35 says, "Cast not away therefore your confidence, which hath great recompense of reward." When you continue faithfully obeying Him, and relying upon His grace, you will receive what is reserved for you. He is full of rich rewards and committed to seeing them established in your life.

But an exhortation in 2 John 8 is of vital importance: "Look to yourselves, that we lose not those things which we have wrought, but that we receive a full reward."

You risk losing the ground you have gained, unless you stay in the things you have learned. If you can retain the faith and grace you have grown into, you will continue to receive the fullness of His will and the rewards of His promised abundance.

The same warning is found in Hebrews 12:15: "Looking diligently lest any man fail of the grace of God; lest any root of bitterness springing up trouble you, and thereby many be defiled."

The word *fail* is to become deficient or *to lack*. It requires diligence to stay sufficient in

God's grace. You must continue to enter His presence and have a fresh deposit of His grace active within your heart.

Deprived of that growth in grace, you will have undesirable roots begin to grow and defile, or contaminate, the pure power of His presence.

Not only are you changed when grace fades in you, but the ones you influence may be contaminated by the bitter results you experience.

Those who have a heart to follow God's lead must be diligent to keep themselves focused upon His grace.

Grace grows as you come before the throne of God and enter His presence. There you must absorb His love and attitude. You take on His character and compassion. He will impart to you His very heart to share with others.

It is in this new relationship of following Jesus that you keep yourself strong and secure. You will live by the strength of His deposits within your heart. They are deposits of His character that, when nurtured, become the fruit of the Spirit flowing out of your inner being.

Again to the Galatians, the Apostle Paul describes these expressions of the Spirit life: "But the fruit of the Spirit is love, joy, peace, patience, kindness, goodness, faithfulness, gentleness, self-control..." (Galatians 5:22-23, NAS).

The real question is, do we really want to follow Him? Do we honestly want His will? Will we turn from manipulating for what we want—to trusting Him and His ways?

Most would deny that they are going their own way. But precious few are actually being led by God in the paths of righteousness. Isaiah 53:6 says: "All of us like sheep have gone astray, each of us has turned to his own way; but the Lord has caused the iniquity of us all to fall on Him" (NAS).

Jesus has given you an entrance to the throne of grace to obtain all the strength and resources you need. Enter by faith and receive from Him. He reaches out to pick you up if you have fallen from grace.

5

Stewards of God's Grace

The grace of God is such a vast subject that scholars have filled volumes in examining its aspects. Every believer, however, needs to know the special ways that God's grace is essential to living and growing in the midst of our circumstances.

One of my priorities has always been that the truths from God's Word bring an impact into a person's situation. Truth which cannot be implemented and experienced is of no more value than error.

An important truth about grace is found in 1 Peter 4:10-11(NEB):

Whatever gift each of you may have received, use it in service to one another, like good stewards dispensing the grace of God in its varied forms. Are you a speaker? Speak as if you uttered oracles of God. Do you give service? Give it as

in the strength which God supplies.
In all things so act that the glory may
be God's through Jesus Christ; to
him belong glory and power for ever
and ever. Amen.

A steward administers or exercises
responsible care over possessions entrusted
to him. The thought of being a steward over
anything does not carry a great excitement
or sense of outstanding importance. It seems
very common and mundane. But steward-
ship is really the day-to-day establishing of
God's ways and manner in His kingdom.
You must do His will, His way, or it will
never become established in you.

As a believer, you have been entrusted
with God's grace. It is a power placed within
your heart to sustain you and influence you.
Second Peter 1:3 says He has deposited all
things that pertain to life and godliness
within your heart. His grace is there to
empower you to fulfill all He has called you
to do.

The wise steward of grace is to faithfully
distribute God's gifts to meet needs. It is not
to meet his own needs alone, but to become
a vessel of God's divine flow into others.

Within every true believer's heart is the desire to be used by God in showing His goodness and His might against the devil's works. The real richness of the Christian life is in having God's great delivering power flow through you.

Remember, grace is the kindness of a master toward his inferiors or servants. So it is clearly grace which God has toward mankind. But—according to Thayer's Greek-English lexicon of the New Testament—it is also His merciful kindness, exerting His holy influence upon us to turn us, keep us, strengthen us and increase us in His ability to do His will.

In Acts 6:8 notice, "And Stephen, full of grace and power, was performing great wonders and signs among the people" (NAS).

It was grace and power that made Stephen stand head and shoulders above others. Grace empowered him to move with God and bring wonders and signs of God's anointing. It will put you into that kind of life, if you act wisely as its steward.

The Apostle Peter described this grace as having various aspects. The *King James*

Version translates it as the "manifold grace of God" in 1 Peter 4:10.

Notice *The Amplified Bible* translation of this verse: "As each of you has received a gift (a particular spiritual talent, a gracious divine endowment), employ it for one another as [befits] good trustees of God's many-sided grace—faithful stewards of the extremely diverse [powers and gifts granted to Christians by] unmerited favor."

Each of us has received a gift from God. It is not only the gift of grace and salvation, but also a specific facet of His own grace to work in us and reveal His greatness.

The word translated *gift* in the New Testament is a gift of grace, according to Thayer. The root word in Greek is *grace* and really indicates the results of grace. So the various gifts named in the New Testament can be understood as "gifts of grace."

It is easy to grasp this concept when you consider them separately. Each is an area that needs God's influence and empowering to function.

First Corinthians 12 lists nine gifts of the Holy Spirit that will flow through Christians to enable them to minister effectively. They are manifestations of the Spirit of God in power, revelation and utterance.

But other gifts are mentioned in the New Testament. In Romans 12:6, the Apostle Paul says, "Having then gifts differing according to the grace that is given to us..." He then proceeds to list seven gifts of grace in which some will function.

In Ephesians 4:7 Paul says, "Naturally there are different gifts and functions; individually grace is given to us in different ways out of the rich diversity of Christ's giving" (Phillips, 1960 edition).

Verse 11 adds, "And He Himself gave some to be apostles, some prophets, some evangelists, and some pastors and teachers" (NKJV). These are gift ministries to the Body of Christ for equipping and maturing the Church.

There is yet another list of gifts in 1 Corinthians 12:28: "And God has appointed these in the church: first apostles, second prophets, third teachers, after that miracles, then gifts of healings, helps, administrations, varieties of tongues" (NKJV).

These gifts are not named in some order of importance or authority that places apostles at the top of God's list. Rather, they appear in an order of function in His plan. All have the same standing in the kingdom of God. Every person has been bought with the same price and holds the same place of importance in the Father's heart.

Scripture refers to more than 20 different gifts, all of them the outward workings of the godly influence within the hearts of God's people.

To be a true steward of God's grace, you must understand not only the grace given to every believer, but also the unique calling and gifting of the Holy Spirit for each life.

We are not all the same nor are we called to be clones of some superstar in Christianity. We each are in Christ and must cultivate our place of service to Him.

When this becomes real to you, the importance of the various positions in the Body of Christ will be easy to appreciate. The gift speaks more of the One Who gave it than the one who now possesses it. God's gifts in a person really point to Him. They testify to His ability to do extraordinary things through ordinary people.

This frees us from the destructive trap of comparison and competition. We are not in a race against others in the kingdom of God, and we must not measure our success or failure by the abilities or grace in others. If I belong to God, then I must serve Him.

In 2 Corinthians 10:12, the Apostle Paul said, "For we dare not class ourselves or compare ourselves with those who commend themselves. But they, measuring themselves by themselves, and comparing themselves among themselves, are not wise" (NKJV).

Significance is not in how big or small my contribution may seem, but rather in the One Who has told me to do what I do. If I can be confident that I am following the voice of the Lord that is all the significance I need.

When Paul speaks of the calling of God which is on every person, he brings into perspective the reason for it. Notice 1 Corinthians 1:26-29 (NKJV):

> For you see your calling, brethren, that not many wise according to the flesh, not many mighty, not many noble, are called. But God has chosen

the foolish things of the world to put to shame the wise, and God has chosen the weak things of the world to put to shame the things which are mighty; and the base things of the world and the things which are despised God has chosen, and the things which are not, to bring to nothing the things that are, that no flesh should glory in His presence.

Clearly, it is not achievements or personality that God is looking for, but simply someone who will say yes to Him. He receives glory because we make ourselves available to Him.

When I realized that God had called me and others because of His plan, and not because of some mystical quality, I knew I could be used by Him. I could meet the qualification and have the heart to follow Him.

The calling of God and service to Him are not confined to what is done in a church service or evangelistic meeting. Each of the many gifts and graces is a vital aspect of the ministry of the gospel.

Whether the ministry is in administration or giving or helps, it is important to see that God will use all to His glory.

Many Christian parents have pushed a child to be a pastor or preacher without really knowing from the Holy Spirit that it is God's will. They have assumed that these ministries must be the highest calling. If the child is not truly called by God to that life, however, he will struggle to fulfill his parents' expectations, but never discover God's true desire for himself.

How can you succeed when you are following the wrong voice? That is just as destructive as the father who will hear of nothing for his child but medical school or law school.

When parents see their child's future only through the eyes of their own ambitions, they set a course for trouble. Proverbs 22:6 says, "Train up a child in the way he should go: and when he is old, he will not depart from it." It is important that it is the way *he* should go—not only the way a parent wishes he would go.

A spouse can be guilty of the same mistake. I have seen many men who struggled with failure after failure in an area of ministry to which they were not called. Their wives were sure that was the only way their husbands could be honorable

Christians. But these women frustrated the grace of God and themselves.

On the other hand, a person can be discouraged from the work God has for him or her when well-meaning Christians are unable to picture that person in a full-time ministry.

As a young Christian, I knew I was called to the ministry where I function today. I began to prepare myself in the best way I knew, through prayer and the study of Scripture.

One day I went to my pastor and told him my belief that I was called to be a minister of the gospel. I will never forget his response: "Dennis, not everyone is called to be a minister." He gave me no encouragement whatsoever. I know I did not look like a candidate for the ministry in most people's eyes, but I knew in my heart it was right.

Some months later, God led me to another church where the pastor saw beyond appearances and helped me grow into the calling of God.

Even then, a wonderful Christian businessman came to me with some advice. "Dennis, the world does not need another preacher," he said. "What is needed are godly businessmen." Then he wanted to help me step into his idea for my life.

If you will embrace the grace in which you are to walk, and if you will be a wise steward over it, you will flourish in the direction God takes you. It will be accompanied by a peaceful and satisfied soul.

When you are at peace in His grace, you can distribute it to others as a faithful steward. This is at the heart of true Christian fellowship.

Fellowship is more than shaking hands and chatting—much more. It is becoming involved with the situations people are facing.

In Acts 2:42 we have a revealing glimpse of the emerging Church and the priorities of its people: "And they continued steadfastly in the apostles' doctrine and fellowship, in the breaking of bread, and in prayers" (NKJV).

Fellowship is involvement. It is literally partnership and participation. One person joins with another to stand with him and see a situation turned around.

You can impart the grace within you to lift those you meet: "Let no corrupt communication proceed out of your mouth, but what is good for necessary edification, that it may impart grace to the hearers" (Ephesians 4:29, NKJV).

Your words will carry the grace deposited in you and plant it in the heart of the one with whom you come in fellowship.

The more you nurture the grace and gifts you have received, the greater your impact will be and the broader your influence will become. Your service to God will become evident in your serving His grace to those around you.

Let God's grace be established in your heart, and you will be free to flourish.

6

Shout Grace to the Mountain

Zerubbabel was the godly governor over Judah. One of the greatest challenges of his life came when King Cyrus of Persia commissioned him to oversee the rebuilding of the temple in Jerusalem.

Though Zerubbabel had been honored with a very important task, he knew that he needed the words of God's prophet to take hold of his position with confidence. The prophet Zechariah assured him:

> ...This is the word of the Lord unto Zerubbabel, saying, Not by might, nor by power, but by my Spirit, saith the Lord of hosts. Who art thou, O great mountain? before Zerubbabel thou shalt become a plain: and he shall bring forth the headstone thereof with shoutings, crying, Grace, grace unto it (Zechariah 4:6-7).

God was seeking a man who would rely upon Him for the ability and wisdom to fulfill His plans. He was not looking for one with the might or the power in himself to try to accomplish God's will.

What we do in God's kingdom that will remain and bear fruit will be by the Spirit of God and not by human effort alone. As the saying goes, God is looking not for ability, but for availability. He searches for those whose hearts are turned toward Him and want only to please and obey Him.

Even with an obedient heart, many times a mountain seems to stand between you and where you know God wants you. Like Zerubbabel, you may have been commissioned to do a job or make a personal change—or even build a building. But there can be very real roadblocks in your path.

God's plans can seem overwhelming from the human point of view. If you focus on your own lack of ability, you will see only mountains. You must see through the eyes of God's Word and promise in order to stretch beyond the limits of your ability, and draw instead upon the resource of His ability.

Romans 5:2 says, "By whom also we have access by faith into this grace wherein we stand, and rejoice in hope of the glory of God."

We reach into increasing levels of God's grace by faith in His Word. It takes vision and faith in God to really grasp and begin to act on His Word and commands for our life. We must see ourselves in the light of His grace working in us and through us.

We must see beyond the limitations of our experience or education. As vital as these qualities are, they can betray us by restricting our willingness to trust Him in unfamiliar areas and situations.

Notice in Zechariah 4:7, God asked, "*Who* is that mountain?" The "who" may be well-meaning people or even our own way of thinking. It is not always problems from an enemy that we struggle with. The obstacle for many who would do wonderful things in God's kingdom is their own sense of inadequacy.

Remember, however, God is not really looking for the *great* to do His work. He looks for the *willing*. When a devoted and willing heart yields to Him, the grace to accomplish His plans will become more and more evident.

With the commission to build, Zerubbabel received the direction and promise of how this temple would be completed. Look at Zechariah 4:6-7, (TLB):

> Not by might, nor by power, but by my Spirit, says the Lord Almighty - you will succeed because of my Spirit, though you are few and weak. Therefore no mountain, however high, can stand before Zerubbabel! For it will flatten out before him! And Zerubbabel will finish building this Temple with mighty shouts of thanksgiving for God's mercy, declaring that all was done by grace alone.

You must realize that God is committed to your success. He will unleash within you all that is needed to finish the task you face. But it will be done in strict adherence to His Word and His plan.

He says you can succeed because of the Spirit of God within you, regardless of your sense of weakness. He has said, "...let the weak say, I am strong" (Joel 3:10).

The mountain that stands before you can become flat, and you can move ahead unhindered by your own weakness or the attacks of the devil.

You will finish the job that God has given you, and you will do it declaring that all was done by grace alone.

Grace is God's empowering within your heart to do what you cannot do alone. When problems or insufficiency seem to stand in your way like a mountain, His grace keeps you strong and moving ahead into His perfect plan.

Faith in God removes the mountains. *Grace* keeps the mountains from moving you.

This grace from God can grow and even multiply in your heart. Second Peter 3:18 tells us to grow in grace. In the epistles, Paul begins his letters with, "Grace be multiplied to you." James 4:6 tells us, "...He giveth more grace."

You must activate and develop this grace. The prophet said he would shout, "Grace, grace," to the mountain. When you increase inside, a greater influence can flow out from you to change things. First you are changed, then you can bring change to situations.

The influence of truth from God's Word will create the power to bring change. It is not truth alone, however, that brings change, but rather truth that has become a part of your life.

A.W. Tozer said it this way: "Truth that is not experienced is no better than error, and just as dangerous."

You can see this in John 1:

In him was life; and the life was the light of men. And the light shineth in darkness; and the darkness comprehended it not...and of His fullness have all we received, and grace for grace. For the law was given by Moses, but grace and truth came by Jesus Christ (verses 4-5, 16-17).

There is a contrast here between the law given by Moses and the truth which came by the Lord Jesus.

Though the law was truth, it produced no power for those who were under it. The people were helpless to fulfill the law, because of the strength of sin within them.

The truth which Jesus brought, however, was revealed with a power to live in the revealed truth. Grace was given to empower those under the law of the New Covenant. Now all who will receive Him will receive His grace that makes them free to fulfill all that the New Covenant says.

Truth without grace brings only law. There is no power to live in the truth. Grace and truth bring the freedom to see the great promises of God's laws working in you and through you.

When you do His work, His way, you will see fruit that remains. If you try to do His will and work in your own strength, and not by His grace, you will fail to obtain the results He has promised.

I must do what I do by the grace of God! The Apostle Paul said, "But by the grace of God I am what I am..." (1 Corinthians 15:10). I too must be what He wants me to be by the grace of God.

In First Corinthians 3:10-13, Paul reveals the importance of this truth:

According to the grace of God which is given unto me, as a wise masterbuilder, I have laid the foundation, and another buildeth thereon. But let every man take heed how he buildeth thereupon. For other foundation can no man lay than that is laid, which is Jesus Christ. Now if any man build upon this foundation gold, silver, precious stones, wood, hay, stubble; every man's work shall be made manifest: for the day shall declare it, because it shall be revealed by fire; and the fire shall try every man's work of what sort it is.

Paul's work was according to the grace which was given to him. We must take heed how we build. Is what we are doing according to grace, or is it our own ideas and fleshly desires?

It is not only what we do, but *how* we do it that is important. Only what is done by God's grace is considered to be gold or silver. All else is dead works that will not survive the fiery trials. Trials will come, but you and your work in the kingdom of God can remain fruitful in the times of testing. Many find that their work really has accomplished nothing, because ambition has moved them, not the Holy Spirit of God.

When the devil's attacks come, you will see how you have been building in the kingdom of God. Many are so dismayed when the fire tries them that they run for shelter.

Others are not moved. They know that setbacks may come, but that they are only temporary. Storms may blow in, but they will blow out again. If your foundation is built by the grace of God, you will be standing when the storm is over.

First John 5:4 says, "For whatsoever is born of God overcometh the world: and this is the victory that overcometh the world, even our faith."

Not only can you overcome, but whatever God has caused to be born in your heart can overcome. *Whatever* is born of God can conquer as well as *whoever*. The key is: What is done must be according to grace.

When Paul faced the threats of Satan's strategies, he called upon God. In 2 Corinthians 12:9, God reveals a powerful principle in His answer to Paul's prayer: "My grace is sufficient for thee: for my strength is made perfect in weakness...."

God's grace is more than enough! The deposit of God in your heart and the ability given you by His grace, are more than enough to overcome Satan's plots. God's strength becomes effective when you recognize your own weakness.

Christianity is continually accepting what you cannot do and what Jesus Christ can do through you.

Again in 1 Corinthians 15:10, the Apostle Paul says, "But by the grace of God I am what I am: and his grace which was bestowed upon me was not in vain; but I laboured more abundantly than they all: yet not I, but the grace of God which was with me."

It was by the grace at work within him that Paul labored. If the Body of Christ would grasp that truth, our effectiveness would increase, and our fleshly ambition would die.

Hebrews 13:9 says, "For it is a good thing that the heart be established with grace...." You are strengthened and made to stand firm by the grace in your heart. It stabilizes you and keeps you from being shaken.

Many years ago when the Holy Spirit began to speak into my heart that He wanted me to write, I remember thinking how strange that He would ask that of me.

I knew so many others who were much more qualified. I felt so lacking in myself to communicate through books. Yet I also knew the voice of the Holy Spirit.

When I discussed this with my wife, Vikki, she was confident that this was what God wanted. She never seemed to waver, though she knew I felt unqualified.

As I continued to seek God and remain open to His leading, I finally agreed that I must begin to write.

I brought the notes of my studies on meditating in God's Word, laid them out on the table along with my Bible and reference books, and began to pray.

I spent the next four days, six hours each day, writing. The result was the first small book we published, titled *How to Meditate God's Word*. Thousands of copies of that book have gone to many nations of the world, bringing that simple truth to many people. It was my decision and labor, but in reality, it was the grace of God from within.

It was then that we realized that the Holy Spirit had made writing a major part of the ministry to which Vikki and I had been called. It was not according to our ability, but rather according to His grace.

God's callings are callings of grace. His gifts of the Holy Spirit are gifts of grace. You can grow in the grace of God and complete all He has desired for you.

"Now I commit you to God and to the word of his grace, which can build you up and give you an inheritance among all those who are sanctified" (Acts 20:32, NIV).

References

The Amplified Bible, New Testament AMP. © 1954, 1958, by the Lockman Foundation, La Habra, California.

Scripture quotations marked HOP are taken from *The Heart of Paul: Biblical Truth in Today's Language, a Relational Paraphrase of the New Testament.* © 1976 by Ben Campbell Johnson. Used by permission of Word Books, Waco, Texas.

The Living Bible (TLB). 1971 by Tyndale House Publishers, Wheaton, Illinois.

Scripture quotations marked NAS are taken from the *New American Standard Bible.* © The Lockman Foundation 1960, 1962, 1963, 1968, 1971, 1972, 1973, 1975, 1977. Used by permission.

Scripture quotations marked NEB are taken from *The New English Bible.* © The Delegates of the Oxford University Press and The Syndics of the Cambridge University Press 1961, 1970. Reprinted by permission.

Dennis Burke has affected thousands of people through a refreshing approach to God's Word and the power of the Holy Spirit. His ministry takes him to a different part of the United States almost every week, as well as to Australia, Asia, New Zealand, Canada and the United Kingdom.

Dennis began as an associate pastor and youth minister in Southern California. There he obtained great insight into the work of the local church. In 1976, he and his wife, Vikki, moved to Fort Worth, Texas, to work with Kenneth Copeland. After two years, God led him to enter his own ministry.

Dennis is the author of several books, including *How to Meditate God's Word* and *Knowing God Intimately*. He also serves the International Convention of Faith Ministries as International Director and Trustee.

The simplicity and balance with which Dennis teaches bring powerful insight for successful Christian living.

OTHER BOOKS BY DENNIS BURKE

You Can Conquer Life's Conflicts

Knowing God Intimately

Rewards of the Diligent

The Law of the Wise

How to Meditate God's Word
also available in Spanish

Yielding to the Holy Spirit

Additional copies of this book or the
above listed books, are available from
your local bookstore or by writing:

Dennis Burke
P.O. Box 150043
Arlington, Texas 76015

*Please include your prayer requests and
comments when you write.*